GW00391253

Topsham
Past and Present

Chips Barber

Illustrations by
Andrea Barber

OBELISK PUBLICATIONS

We have over 200 Devon titles. For a current list, please send SAE to
Obelisk Publications, 2 Church Hill, Pinhoe, Exeter, EX4 9ER, Tel: (01392) 468556

All Drawings and Cover by Andrea Barber

First published in 1994, reprinted in 1997 and 2004 by
Obelisk Publications, 2 Church Hill, Pinhoe, Exeter, Devon
Designed by Chips and Sally Barber
Printed in Great Britain by
Avocet Press, Cullompton, Devon

© Chips Barber/Obelisk Publications

2

ℭopsham
Past and Present

Topsham will never really be part of Exeter. It has its own special atmosphere and community spirit; it is a place with its own identity and history; and it is fiercely protective of its heritage, customs and characters. Put boundaries where you will, it won't make a scrap of difference: 'Topsam folk' are not Exonians!

They say a view over water will add thousands to a property's value; well, they don't come much better than the estuary views at Topsham. People come from all over the world to photograph a sunset from the top of the church steps – a Topsham kind of magic!

Away from this view, the town is a maze of narrow streets, courts and passageways. With its tight thoroughfares Topsham is not custom-built to accommodate the motor car, which is a problem that has dogged the town in a number of ways over recent years.

Although the town gets visitors, it is not really a tourist place; most people choose to visit the nearby cathedral city of Exeter, some three or four miles upriver. People who pass through on the railway to Exmouth are also denied the pleasures of 'the best bits' of this riverside settlement, whilst anyone who zooms down the M5 sees nothing – unless their vehicle is tall enough for occupants to see over the barriers!

This book came about for a number of reasons. Local folk are obviously interested in their own area, and many years ago I was involved in the production of Sara Vernon's *Talking about Topsham*, which was very well received. But Roy Wheeler, who loves Topsham and knows the place intimately, agreed there was scope for a more general 'guide', and supplied many of the stories in this book. This time I wanted to show some of the other aspects of the estuary town, not least its buildings: some quite grand, others more modest. As my daughter, just sixteen years old at the time, was looking for an outlet for her pencil sketches, she needed very little encouragement to illustrate this book.

Having listed enough reasons why this little book has been put together, let's see what surprises await us in a town so proud of its roots...

As a port of past importance Topsham has a variety of building styles almost unmatched in Devon. The nearest to it I have seen is Appledore, but that is much smaller than Topsham. Like its North Devon counterpart, Topsham is still a place of sights and smells. Perhaps these are not as many, or as diverse, as 'in the good old days', but they are enough to create the unique charm that is 'Topsam'. The late, great historian, W. G. Hoskins, wrote: *"It is quite the most rewarding small town in Devon... and probably one of the most interesting in England. The whole feeling of the waterfront is remarkable: the decaying shipyards, the rotting hulks in the river mud, the derelict warehouses, nail factories, and quays, the multitudinous cats, the wonderful river views... no wonder Topsham has been a favourite walk for Exeter people since the eighteenth century..."*

But that was written some fifty years ago; although the cats still prowl around the alleys and peer out of the attractive riverside gardens, many of the disused warehouses have gone or been adapted for other uses. What was once a prison is now the custodian of reproduction furniture. Some of the pubs, where seafaring folk temporarily forgot the dangers of their perilous profession, have adapted to other uses. Even the signal box at the station has fulfilled other purposes: a far cry from its control of seaside-bound trains and lurching-landward locomotives.

Topsham has far more pubs than it really deserves for its size of population. Here we consider some of them, whilst not forgetting the ones that have finally 'called time'.

The town is built on a red ridge set between the rivers Clyst and Exe, which unite just to the south of the town. The latter, until the M5 road bridge was built, was generally regarded as too wide to bridge. However, the Clyst, despite also being tidal, is a more modest flow and a bridge has straddled it for centuries. Sited on the Topsham side of the Clyst, the Bridge Inn has also been there for centuries. Listed as an ancient monument, it is a remarkable pub with a distinctive character. In the days of smuggling, peepholes enabled the occupants to keep a watchful eye out for any customs officers. The building is intricate, and well blessed for stowing away illicitly imported goods, notably tobacco and brandy. Topsham being a smuggler's paradise, the local populace were more than familiar with this sort of trade. The pub is believed to be haunted, as befits a building of its age; the ghost in this case stays well out of sight, but occasionally tosses the odd beer mat in the air.

4

In late March 1998, the pub entertained a very famous guest: the Queen. She was on her way to the Royal Marine Camp at Lympstone, when she 'popped in'. She was presented with some bottles of anniversary ale, which had been brewed to commemorate 101 years of family involvement with the Bridge Inn. It is believed to be the first time Her Majesty has ever been photographed in a public house.

On the opposite side of the River Clyst is Fisher's Bridge Mill. A two-storey stone tide mill, it was worked until 1960 when the machinery was taken out and its mill pool filled in.

The Malt Scoop Inn in White Street is one of the many pubs to have ceased trading. It was once the smallest pub in Exeter with a tiny serving area. It closed in the 1980s despite a fight to keep it open. There were rumours of drinking after hours – this was in the days when licensing hours were less flexible than of late – and a watch was kept on this diminutive place of refreshment. When the long arm of the law called late one evening, in anticipation of catching some after-hours revellers, an inordinately long wait ensued before the door was unbolted. Surprise, Surprise! There was nobody there. Surely the Topsham tipplers did not avail themselves of the opportunity afforded by a bolt hole into the kitchen of an adjacent property?

This part of Topsham was once regarded as the rough quarter, but times have changed. In the past many of the town's fishermen lived either in White Street or Shapter Street, and street fights, after serious drinking sessions, used to be the norm on Saturday nights. One tough old character, Jimmy Luxon, fought just for the hell of it. He would throw down the challenge by tossing his hat in the air, the person retrieving it knowingly taking the opportunity for a good scrap. The battle-worn Jimmy Luxon had a gruesome end when he hanged himself along 'Serrallicks Walk'. Another character suffered from delusions when he got drunk, and would try to fight with his shadow all the way home, whilst another old boozer would lean on a wall on the left-hand side of the street and use it to guide him home some 70 yards away.

However, even more outrageous occurrences plagued the London and South Western (now Drakes); the pub made national news headlines when, apparently, the pub and all its regulars were transported up to that final frontier known as space. There was even talk of Martians. Before you get more carried away than all those involved, the report appeared in the *Sunday Sport*!

The inns of Topsham have not been without their share of adversity. The Lighter, whose name is derived from a type of flat-bottomed boat used to unload cargoes from vessels moored out in the estuary, was the victim of a terrible fire on 4 May 1971. I remember this former Customs House as a much smaller and poorly illuminated pub, despite its name. It had a blazing fire, but this was nowhere near as spectacular as the fire that wrecked it on that fateful late spring night. But it has risen, like the Phoenix from the ashes. It is an attractive, well-located pub, although it has changed hands, for various reasons, several times.

Many years ago, when the local football team played their matches at Bowling Green Marshes, they used to get changed at the Lighter, then come back to the pub for a dunk in the old metal bath tub. The referee also changed here, so, if Topsham had lost, the journey back from the pitch was potentially

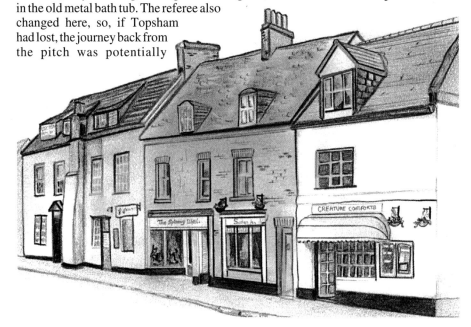

eventful for the official; it was not uncommon for him to have a close encounter with the famous Topsham mud, or be garlanded in a mantle of seaweed!

Adjoining the quayside, at the rear of what is now part of the present pub, were premises used by Trout's Boatbuilders. They were not only masters of their art, but also experts on gauging the width between the pillars. Time after time they would build a craft to within a whisker's width of being able to get it out once it was complete. Often onlookers congregated to see if a vessel would get wedged, but it never did!

The Passage House Inn, in Ferry Road, is a favourite of many people, particularly on a fine summer's evening when it is possible to sit in the beer garden to enjoy one of those famous Topsham sunsets over the hills beyond Whitestone. In January 1939 the landlady, Mrs Davies, had a lucky escape when a 30-foot stone wall at the back of the inn suddenly collapsed, bringing down 150 tons of earth and rubble. The damage was

extensive, but nobody was harmed. The fall was blamed on a combination of wet weather and frequent, intermittent frosts, conditions that are also capable of breaking up road surfaces and hastening the demise of similarly insecure structures.

Another former Topsham alehouse, the Railway Inn, collapsed one Sunday night. This time, however, the demise of the pub was not attributed to a pattern of weather conditions, nor to any structural weaknesses in the fabric of the building. No, there was only one culprit: the Devil! Although this is not a reason recommended for putting down on any insurance claim, there were witnesses! Ignoring the spirit of the Sabbath, a number of men were playing cards in the inn when one of them bent down to retrieve a card that had fallen onto the floor. According to various accounts, the man found that his hand was pinned to the floor by the Devil. A frantic struggle followed until the man's friends freed him from his predicament. The occupants of the inn then took flight, just before the end wall of the pub collapsed! Although the building was repaired, it was never again licensed for spirits.

One building not troubled like this is the sixteenth-century Globe Hotel, although to look at it, it has all the atmosphere necessary to merit a few spooks. The oldest document found, so far, relating to this inn, is dated 1700; it links it to the King John, which used to be located in South Street, Exeter, and was another hostelry run by the same owner. The name is derived from the symbol of Portuguese wine merchants (a globe), which presumably shows the far-reaching range of their interests. On the outside of the hotel is a three-legged emblem, a sign of the Cycle Touring Club who would have used this lovely old coaching inn às one of their regular stops. At one time the hotel was run by a man called Radford who was politically motivated: if he didn't like your politics, he would refuse to serve you! Behind the Globe used to be Rodd's Field, named after a local butcher.

In 1962 Arthur Wilde wrote an article about Topsham. He had this to say of the nearby Salutation, when considering what it was like in the middle of the nineteenth century:

James Moore kept the Salutation Hotel and posting-house in the High Street. This old coaching inn dates back to the year 1720, and whenever I see it I am reminded of the old tradition of English comfort, warmth, good food, and jovial company for travellers at the end of a long journey by horse-drawn coach.

Here I can imagine the arrival of Mr Pickwick and Sam Weller, passing through those large oaken doors, panelled and studded, and being received by the waiter, wearing knee-breeches and coloured waistcoat, with the usual napkin over his arm.

Sometimes I go through those massive old doors to the old bowling green at the rear, with its old pavilion and the apple trees nearby. The other day I was told by a native that he thought the last time that bowling green was played on was about 45 years ago [about 1917]. At the Salutation he used to play skittles and he had known dancing to take place when bowling had finished there. He also mentioned the hotel ballroom.

Topsham Past and Present

Well, they say it takes two to tango, and wrestling was also in evidence at the Salutation in the past. This was not the 'entertaining' variety of the sport that graces our television screens today, but an ultra macho and totally serious struggle, which attracted large crowds. One of the greatest exponents of this form of wrestling was Abraham Cann. He came from Colebrooke, near Crediton, and became the champion of England in 1827. It was believed that this man of

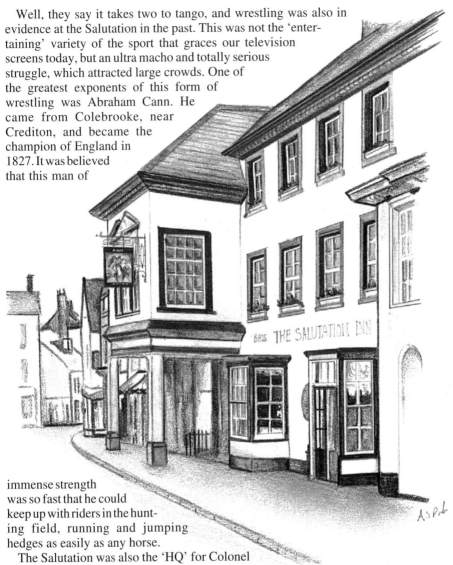

immense strength was so fast that he could keep up with riders in the hunting field, running and jumping hedges as easily as any horse.

The Salutation was also the 'HQ' for Colonel Robert Hall's Devon and Cornwall Fencibles. These were raised in 1794 in order to keep a vigilant eye on the coastline, the worry being a possible invasion by the French. Although this group existed for only eight years, their colours are on the South Transept of the nearby St Margaret's Church.

The King's Head was built in the eighteenth century, but was modernised and renovated in 1930. The building, like many in the Topsham area, includes bricks that were made in Holland and carried as ballast on trading ships. Long ago it was a pub favoured by shipwrights, so the conversation then was highly influenced by tales of the sea.

The Double Locks Hotel, on the Exeter Canal, is also made of these 'clinkers'. Clearly the Dutch House, in Topsham, a grade two listed property, falls into that category. Holland was the largest outlet for the serges produced in Devon, and Topsham merchants plied the route to the low country so often that they were influenced by the buildings they saw. Many of them date from the period 1700–30. The grandness of many of these 'Dutch' houses was a reflection of the prosperity of the port at that time.

Several of Topsham's pubs were involved in a celebration of an historic episode in the town's colourful past. Monmouth Street and Monmouth Hill derive their names from a visit in 1685 by James Scott, better known as the Duke of Monmouth, who at the age of 36 made an unsuccessful bid to take the throne of England. He landed at Lyme Regis, and raised an army to help him in his cause. He was warmly received at Topsham before going on to an overwhelming defeat on the Somerset Levels at Sedgemoor.

The notorious Judge Jeffreys sentenced to death 320 of his accomplices, whilst Monmouth himself was beheaded on Tower Hill, in London.

It was probably at Monmouth House that he addressed the people of Topsham.

In 1985 it was decided to commemorate the tercentenary of this visit. 'The Monmouth Junket' was a colourful event, a pageant involving a lot of people. The idea was the work of Jane Powell, a former director of the Northcott Theatre in Exeter, and local man Griff Thomas. Naturally there was a theatrical element to the proceedings, and the 'Duke of Monmouth' was 'resurrected' for the day, in all his regal finery. The Duke paraded from the Recreation Field along Ferry Road, where he entered the Passage Inn to have 'a stirrup cup' before strolling to Church Steps. Here a local fisherman presented the Duke with a salmon. After climbing the steps, the Duke was greeted by the choir, who sang to him in the churchyard. Next stop was the Salutation, where the Ceremony of the Glove was re-enacted; it was believed that the real Duke of Monmouth had done this very thing 300 years earlier. The specially embroidered glove, by Judy Yeo, was placed on the end of a pole.

A similar tradition is associated with the celebration of market days when traders enjoyed certain concessions; locals extended this to incorporate various revels, often in the knowledge that they could indulge without risk of legal reprimand.

Meanwhile, the Duke, 1985-style, moved on to the Lighter. Here, between this pub and the Steam Packet opposite, he was presented with a pineapple. In Monmouth Street the Duke witnessed a street party in his honour. There were other activities, which included a period play and a craft market, to round off a memorable day, one which presented a history lesson in an imaginative and entertaining way.

The Lord Nelson is named after another character from history, a man who was very familiar with Devon for a number of reasons! The pub's appearance has changed beyond recognition in recent years. Many years ago it used to have a trough and a pump. Local lads would wait for 'brakes', or horse-drawn carriages, to arrive, then, as the trough emptied, would pump more in to keep it topped up. For this service pennies were thrown at them, and a frantic struggle ensued to see who was game enough to get them.

Opposite there was a sweet shop called Mitchell's, where the triumphant coin-scramblers could swiftly spend their windfall before it burnt a hole in their pockets!

Next door to the pub was a little hall where the Rombolo Minstrels often entertained the local populace with their inimitable brand of entertainment. They would do the old soft shoe shuffle whilst painted in the customary black and white associated with such entertainers. This group included well-known locals such as George Cooksley, Sammy Williams and Edgar ('Zony') Osborne.

The Lord Nelson's central position in Topsham meant that it was well located for the staging of fairs and markets. Henry III gave Topsham a charter to hold a three-day fair on the feast of St Margaret of Antioch. The theory was that if you could sustain such an event over that length of time, you had the right to call your settlement a town.

Events like this had obvious historical roots, just as the wassailing ceremony did in Topsham. Until 1936 it was customary for several Topsham men to carry their shotguns to Shapter Street to the gardens belonging to Messrs G. H. May & Sons. As they walked through the orchard, they discharged their guns at regular intervals, the reverberating noise bouncing around nearby narrow streets loudly enough to wake the dead! 'Wassailing the

Apple Trees' was a custom usually associated with Christmas Eve, or the eve of Twelfth Night. It was carried out with great ritual to ensure a good crop for the next season. At Topsham the ceremony has died out, but elsewhere, notably in the chief cider growing county of Somerset, it is still celebrated.

The Steam Packet is Topsham's second oldest hostelry, but originally was called the Red Lion. Behind it is Amity Place, which was Red Lion Court. The pub is named after a steam packet called 'The Zephyr'. In the past it brewed all its own beer at the back. It was one of two places owned by Charlie Gale, the other being the London & South

Western (now Drakes). He married Tryphena Sparks, one time girlfriend of Thomas Hardy. She was a lady who devoted much energy towards improving the lot of the fishermen. They appreciated everything that she did for them, so, when she died, at a fairly young age, they afforded her the honour of carrying her coffin at her funeral. Thomas Hardy came to Topsham for this sad occasion; he is believed to have left in a flood of tears.

'Punch Miller', who was not named for his pugilistic prowess, but more for his resemblance to Judy's associate, lived near the Steam Packet. He kept his horse and cart opposite the pub. He was seen all over Topsham collecting rubbish, as this was how he earned his living.

Near this pub is a barn said to be the oldest in England.

There have been many other pubs that have come, served their purpose, then disappeared: the Honest Heart became a drill hall; the Ship Aground well and truly foundered to become a bakery (this was the birthplace of the late Morice Parsons, a Topsham Councillor for many years), today it is the Ship Aground Gallery; the Sun set to became a butcher's shop; the Seven Stars, a former cider house, close to the southern end of the churchyard, has a splendid sign showing the celebrated sunset behind the Haldon Hills; the Commercial (previously the Lamb); the Duke of Monmouth; the Ferry; the Five Sealers; the Topsham; and the Welcome, notorious for its bruising and brawling; they have long gone into the annals of social (sometimes antisocial!) history.

This leads us on to that other institution known for its 'tender loving care'…

The police station at Topsham must have been a lively place at times! Number 70 Fore Street served this purpose for a while; it was handily situated as a great number of pubs lay within a minute's walk. It was built in 1791, originally as a Market House with an open ground floor and seven hollow brick arches, but was altered in 1867 to allow the law to be administered in its constabularian way. Part of the building was used as a constable's house. The cells are still at the back of the property, and the 'Charge Room' has now been incorporated, somewhat arrestingly, into a private dwelling. The Central Garage stands on the site of the former market.

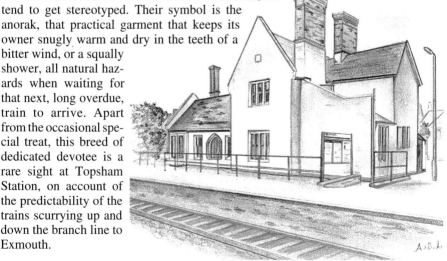

Train enthusiasts are often the butt of comedians, and tend to get stereotyped. Their symbol is the anorak, that practical garment that keeps its owner snugly warm and dry in the teeth of a bitter wind, or a squally shower, all natural hazards when waiting for that next, long overdue, train to arrive. Apart from the occasional special treat, this breed of dedicated devotee is a rare sight at Topsham Station, on account of the predictability of the trains scurrying up and down the branch line to Exmouth.

A.S.B.

But the station has had its moments; if its signal box could talk, it could tell of the days when 40 trains passed through as part of a busy schedule, the level crossing gates opening and shutting with alarming regularity. A wheel in the signal box wound them open.

For no apparent reason there was a tradition that a large crowd would assemble on the platform on Saturday nights to greet the arrival of the last train from Exmouth. It was believed to be a sign of adulthood when a young Topsham man was considered old enough to visit the resort, then come home on that train.

There were quite a few station staff in those days. However, in 1957 the last goods train passed through; in 1958 the branch line running down to Topsham Quay was removed. (This has become Holman Way, a road that partly relieves the Fore Street.) It was a scene of drama when some trucks ran away down towards the quay. An alert Billy Lawrence saw them, and set off in hot pursuit. Alas, he didn't manage to catch up with them; the trucks went through the turntable at the quay and plummeted into the estuary. In normal circumstances there were devices like steel rods that could be used to permit freewheeling trucks to trundle at a controllable speed, but, on this occasion, they turned out not to be up to the job: the trucks became railway lemmings! Fortunately nobody was hurt. If you have ever ridden a bicycle up Holman Way, you will appreciate that there is a distinct gradient that is almost mountainous by railway standards.

The railway line up to Exeter was made into a single track route in 1973, even though half a million journeys a year, between stations on the Exeter–Exmouth branch, were still being recorded. Subsequently the number of trains dropped, and the station staff 'disappeared'. Railway historians reckon that Topsham has the best preserved Victorian crossing station on the former 'South Western' rail system. The stationmaster's house followed a particular style found on stations the length and breadth of the South Western network.

The signal box was given a new, but short, lease of life in 1990 when a young local business man took out a lease to run his business selling mobile phones and office equipment from it. It is a bit like Dr Who's 'Tardis' in that it has much more space than one would imagine, some 370 square feet, unbroken save for the original fireplace. When it was written about in the local press, the reporter lapsed into a rally of puns. You can imagine the sort of thing: a business on the right lines ; 'just the ticket'; all the right signals; on the right track; his station in life... And so it went on, a remorseless round of railway-related asides, longer, in fact, than the length of the lease!

The station, though, has still got its lonicera bush with 'Topsham' spelt out. The Allotment Society deserve credit for keeping this worthy tradition alive.

When you read through books of Topsham memories, such as Sara Vernon's *Talking about Topsham*, you get the impression that the people of Topsham were either most unfortunate, or extremely careless in the self-preservation stakes. Poor old Princey Pyle was run down and killed by a train at the railway crossing; another local woman was run down by a rail truck, which resulted in the loss of both her arms; and there are also numerous examples of self-destruction with drownings and entirely avoidable accidents littering the town's past.

From rails to railings! In Ferry Road is Follett Lodge, once the home of one of the greatest legal minds ever to have lived. Sir William Webb Follett was a genius who rose to the position of Attorney-General. Alas, throughout his life he was dogged by ill-health; he passed away at the age of 47, in 1845. Just around the corner, Follett Road is named in his honour. The late Jimmy Smeall, ex-Mayor of Exeter and former Principal of St Luke's College, made Follett Orchard, in this road, his home.

In Ferry Road there is a set of iron railings that most people pass by without noticing. These were salvaged from the tip by the late Bill Little for a mere twenty pounds. Previously they had adorned St Sidwell's Church in Exeter; after the church was bombed during the war, the railings were taken to the dump. Mr Little incorporated them into his home (Ferry House). On them are various initials: the SS stands for St Sidwell, the M for martyr. St Sidwella was a girl whose mother died and whose father remarried an evil woman. So jealous of the pious and good Sidwella was she that she had a man with a scythe lop off Sidwella's head whilst the poor girl knelt in prayer and divine supplication. Where her head fell there arose a powerful spring of water, known as the springs of St Sidwella. Thus the symbols that represent this virtuous lady are a scythe and a spring. A district of Exeter bears her name.

If you lived in a house called 'Furlong', you would imagine that it would be 220 yards, (or 660 feet) long. 'Not so in the case of Topsham! This house, with one of the most enviable positions in the country, is long, but not that long. In a 1935 newspaper feature it is quoted as being 135 feet – some 525 feet short of the mark. However, it was so long that the lady who lived there in the 1930s had to cope with the problem of conveying fuel from one end of the house to the other.

After much thought (and not without a few backaches) she acquired a small wooden truck that she wheeled the length of the 300-year-old building. The reason for its great length, being some seven times its width, is that it was a sail loft. Furlong is easily recognised as it has a figurehead called 'The Centurion' projecting out over the water.

A former owner converted the end nearest Ferry Road into a sort of chapel, and the architecture reflects this. He also installed an organ. This he gave much use, unwittingly entertaining many Topsham children who crouched down to listen to this eccentric's musical renderings.

Another long slim waterfront building is 'Wixels.' It forms a prominent foreground feature when gazing upriver from the vantage point at the top of Church Steps. It was a sail loft and shed for many years, owned by the Holmans, but later it was bought by a German firm called Wigzell, who imported coal. In 1920 it was bought by Tapley Soper, a local solicitor; he added the Dutch gable, converted it into a house, and called it Wixels.

On the opposite side of the narrow Ferry Road is Nail Cellars, a building that has proved to be the most versatile in the town; few can boast of accommodating so many pursuits at different times. Its name derives from the factory here; it had the tremendous

name of Wigzell's Spiral Fluted Nail Company (which evolved into the name of Wixels opposite). In the nineteenth century the West of England Wagon Works was based in the building; since then it has been used by the Salvation Army for meetings, as a cold store, a mini rifle range, and, in part, an art gallery.

In Ferry Road, and along the Topsham waterfront, are several buildings that are made of limestone. This stone was quarried at Berry Head, at the southern extremity of Tor Bay, then brought around the coast and up to Topsham Quay. Its abundance and suitability for easy shipment meant that it was used extensively in the Exeter area, with the construction of limestone warehouses being one of its main uses. One of the closest is the Old Gaol, a building that sits in the divide between Quay Hill and The Strand. Front on it resembles a coffin house; to all intents and purposes, it probably felt like that to those unfortunates who were locked up there whilst awaiting transportation to the penal colonies! The building has had many uses: as a warehouse, a garage, and a retail outlet for tyres, amongst others. Farther along the same block, George Harris, who was succeeded by his son Alf, for many years operated a blacksmith's business .

Farther along the road is yet another of Topsham's old quays. This is Hannaford's Quay, backed by an attractive sequence of buildings, many of which were warehouses in those halcyon days when Topsham was at its peak as a port. In the late nineteenth century, Captain Hannaford lived at number 10. The bricked-up remains of a hoist can be seen on this property.

The ferry across the estuary saves a considerable walk, bike ride or drive, as the nearest practical crossing place over the Exe is the bridge at Countess Wear. To get back to the other side involves a long detour! Of course, if you have already missed the ferry, or timed it wrongly in the past, you will be well aware of the pedestrian-impeding geography of this immediate area. Such an observation makes the toll seem like a bargain.

The ferry has been established for centuries. It is believed that all-powerful monks ran a ferry here on one of their most important routeways from Sherborne Abbey down into the south west peninsular. They held great tracts of land. These included much of the coastline at Beer, in East Devon, where there still are offshore rocks named after this revered abbey. However, more secular ferrymen have earned a living here since the monks relinquished control.

Occasionally Topsham ferrymen have been given scares, the type and nature of the job bringing a range of occupational hazards. When wind, tide, fog and other misbehaved elements are not at their mischievous, meddlesome ways, other ghostly ghouls are sometimes abroad... Take, for instance, one dark and misty evening when most folks were tucked up by a cosy fireside; a voice boomed out from the far side of the river, demanding the services of the ferryman. "Who is it?" the ferryman replied. "Trankmore," came the answer. This sent shivers down the spine of the Topsham man, for everyone knew that Trankmore had been washed overboard in a mid-ocean storm many months previously. Lest he should have a close encounter with a zombie or ghost, the ferryman refused to cross the misty, murky waters to fetch him. But there were other Topsham men present who were built of sterner stuff; they got out the oars, and brought a live and well Captain Trankmore back to his home port.

Miracle of miracles, the captain had indeed been washed overboard from his homeward-bound ship, but he had been washed straight onto the deck of a Dutch East Indiaman bound in the opposite direction! In an ocean of such immense size, particularly with so little traffic in those days, it was simply amazing that two vessels could pass so close without either seeing the other – and at such a crucial moment!

18

On the other side are the Exminster Marshes, an area famed for its wildlife; it is reminiscent of the Somerset Levels, but on a much smaller scale.

The ferry hut on the west bank is a priceless gem of architectural design (the weather would have to be desperately inclement for anyone to seek shelter in it), whilst the one on the Topsham shore is relatively luxurious!

Nearby is Lock Cottage, in a state of apparent dereliction. It is hard to see whether the cottage or the long redundant gates of Topsham Lock are in the worse state of repair. Many years ago Emily Howard grew up here, sharing a childhood with her three sisters and two brothers. A close inspection of the building will convey an impression of just how crowded it must have been. However, she in turn married, and her first two children were born there. Tragedy struck when her husband was killed, so her two sons went back to Lock Cottage to live with their grandmother. She was Mary Howard, and the nature of her lifestyle meant that she was a tough woman. She was the lock-keeper; she executed her duties with a strength and a will that was admired by many. The living room at Lock Cottage was unusual in that it was below the level of the Exeter Canal; it was reached by going down a flight of steps. After periods of heavy rain, it was necessary to sandbag the entrance to keep out floodwater.

The isolated location of Lock Cottage meant amenities that most would take for granted were unavailable. There was no electricity or gas, and, despite the canal, river and floodwaters, there was no water! This had to be fetched from a tap in a courtyard across at Topsham. To supplement their diet, the family went out at low tides in the summer and 'groped' for flatfish. In the Teign Estuary the technique was different; there they 'fluked' for flatfish, that is, they prodded barbed sticks into the sand where the unwitting flatfish lay awaiting a change in the tides.

If you want to stroll up to Countess Wear on the Topsham side (when the tide is out) you will have to walk Sir Alex Walk, which goes from the Recreation Field up to the M5 bridge. It is named after Sir Alex Hamilton (Hamilton Road) who lived at The Retreat. He was born in 1732, and his childhood was spent in poverty. By the time he reached the age of twelve, he had decided to seek pastures new. Some history books say that he sought, and subsequently found, fame and fortune in the West Indies, whilst others say the East Indies. His wealth brought him to Topsham, and into the lap of luxury. He bought The Retreat, a fine mansion that some people thought had been a sugar factory. This, however, was not quite on the same site, being a few yards nearer to Topsham itself. Captain Robert Orme is attributed with this conversion some time before 1775. It's all rather academic now, as in 1938 the mansion was converted into flats.

The riverside walk has attracted other names over the years, mainly as a result of slovenly speaking on behalf of some of the resident population, or too much time spent in the many pubs and cider houses, because it has been 'Shrallicks Walk', and appeared on other documents as 'Serrallick's Walk'. Sir Alex was High Sheriff in 1786, but died in 1809 at the age of 77.

The Turf Hotel is even more isolated than Lock Cottage, but it is well patronised when the weather is fine. It hasn't changed a great deal in appearance since it was designed and built in 1823. This was to tie in with a major extension to the length, depth and width of this canal; the engineer for this was also the architect for the Turf Hotel – James Green. The east wing originally had stables for up to six horses, on a similar basis to its 'brother' the Double Locks Hotel, also on the Exeter Canal, half a mile to the north of the Exeter by-pass. Above the stables at Turf was a loft; this stored hay for the horses that worked the towpaths for the five and a bit miles up to the canal basin at Exeter (James Green 1830).

It is interesting to note that James Green did not originally give much consideration to the sanitary arrangements of the inn, as it was built with only one toilet! However, this did not detract from the popularity of the place, half the fun being in simply getting there.

In the 1930s and '40s, a lot of its trade was made up of Topsham people. Saturday nights were times of high excitement, as everyone let their hair down. It was customary for some ladies to dance on the tables, whilst Minnow Murphy entertained on the piano. These were family affairs, and a convoy of rowing boats descended on The Turf.

The Water Mongoose offers a more sophisticated way of getting there today, and an evening trip along the Canal is one of relaxed enjoyment. It is possible to catch a boat from Exmouth, but first it's necessary to check the times and days of sailing. Just like in the old days, families are encouraged to visit, the beer garden and children's play area being ideal. Walking to it is a good way to summon up a thirst, provided you are confident of walking a straight line on the way home! If you think all the doors and windows are out of alignment, it's not that you are over the limit, for the inn is built on reed beds and the building is slowly making its way to Australia… on the direct route!

Despite the number of pubs, and the undoubted revelry attached to these places of alcoholic refreshment, there are, to balance the equation, quite a few places in the town where people can worship. The most obvious landmark, seen from the water or viewed from Exminster Marshes, is St Margaret's. This church, the fourth to be built against the original, attractive mediaeval red sandstone tower, is located on a red rock bluff, safely above the highest of spring tides. The view from the top of Church Steps is one of the most attractive and open in Devon. Those who stand here to look at the view often do so for many minutes, because there is so much to see, from the movements on the estuary to the towering clouds that dwarf even the distant pine-covered hills of Haldon. The view has been written about many times, most notably by George Gissing in his nineteenth-century book *The Private Papers of Henry Rycroft*. His description of it has drawn people from far and wide. In 1973 Haruo Suzuki, President of one of the big three chemical companies in Japan, travelled thousands of miles having made Rycroft's book one of his favourites. He waited 40 years for the opportunity, and was not disappointed!

The church was rebuilt around 1876–78 and has withstood, more or less, everything that the elements have thrown at it. However, the hurricane of January 1990 uprooted a tree in the grave-yard; as its long established root system had spread over a substantial area, a number of human bones were unceremoniously torn out of the earth. The same storm ripped hundreds of roof-tiles from houses in the town, and scattered them far and wide. Another tree was blown down, blocking the entrance to the Goat Walk, whilst yet another blocked Holman Way.

One tombstone lies cosily tucked away in the lee of the church, even though the deceased lies some distance away in the graveyard. Thomas Randle was a quartermaster, possibly with Nelson at the Battle of Trafalgar. It is believed that this sailor was one of a small group that helped the mortally wounded Admiral below decks. The Topsham Sea Scouts used to acknowledge his deeds in their Trafalgar Day parade. At the Lord Nelson pub the landlord would raise a signal flag – 'England expects' – and then the sea scouts would march to Randle's grave to lay a laurel wreath. This ceremony ceased more than half a century ago. The reason for the gravestone being apart from the grave can be attributed to the use of a sophisticated lawn mower that not only mowed the grass, but poor old Randle's tombstone as well. Once repaired it was thought wiser to put it against the church out of harm's way.

A one-off ceremony at Topsham enabled one local wag to register a witty observation on the proceedings. A funeral procession entering St Margaret's was somewhat slower and apparently more reverential than normal. This was a misconception as the funeral was of a local man of gargantuan proportions. His wooden overcoat (or coffin) could only be described as 'outsize.' The pall-bearers struggled manfully with their cumbersome burden until they got to the church doors, and there the fun began as it took minutes to squeeze it into the church for the service. The deceased had not been a regular churchgoer, so the comment made, "We couldn't get you into church when you were alive, and we can't get you in now you're dead!" just about summed up the situation.

The Methodist church, built by the Holman family, bucks a trend as it is dedicated to a saint, in this case, St Nicholas. It has been called The Church of Seagoing Men; St Nicholas was the patron saint of seafarers on account of a number of miraculous rescues in the Mediterranean in the fourth century. It's designed in an early English style with a wooden roof meant to resemble that of the hull of a boat.

Nearby is a doctor's surgery housed in an unusual building made of limestone and granite, both building materials of proven strength, but with very different properties and originating from entirely different locations. This is in the shell of the former Victorian Methodist church hall.

But sometimes time is a greater innovator of change than religion, and it is practical forces at work, rather than divine ones, that shapes what a place is like. Topsham's maritime influences are there for all to see, but they are very much in a 'watered down' form than two centuries ago when there was a hustle and bustle about this workaday port. Then there was the real feel of a port where the bulk of the people who lived in Topsham worked in Topsham! Schooners, lighters, brigs and barques rolled off the production line with many fine ships coming from numerous yards along the waterline. In addition to the boatyards, slip-ways, quays and docks there were ropewalks, sail-lofts, warehouses and workshops, all heavily involved in allied pursuits. The scene was a hive of industry, and, of, course, there were all the seagoing men from the port. There were those who stayed with inter-coastal trade, those that ventured farther afield to Holland and other Northern European ports, and those who sailed thousands of miles to earn their living from or on the sea.

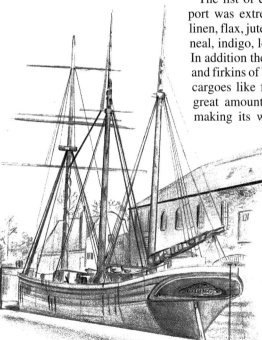

The list of commodities passing through the port was extremely varied; it included wheat, linen, flax, jute, olive oil, shumack, argol, cochineal, indigo, logwood, rags, tar, pitch and iron. In addition there were also leather, paper, flour and firkins of butter. There were more attractive cargoes like fruit and wines, and there was a great amount of wool, somewhat sheepishly making its way out of port. The quays and wharfs would have been a really spectacular sight in Topsham's heyday as a port. But steam came and boats got bigger; as the Exe is not a deep water inlet, ports like Topsham saw a decline set in. It's a very different place today; the waterfront now is a much more domestic and residential scene.

Topsham's fine museum is situated in an old sail-loft, and is well worth a visit for anyone who wants to learn more about the town's past from its exhibits and on-hand experts.

There are still many people around who always refer to this estuary town as 'Topsham-on-the-Mud', at low tide something that would be difficult to deny, as there is an abundance of this soft, oozing substance that makes its own noises whilst supporting a little world of wildlife. Precious stuff indeed. The mud has not escaped the attention of speculators. In my book *The Lost City of Exeter* I wrote about a Henry Phillips from Clyst Honiton, who saw the opportunity to use this as a raw material for making bricks. He launched the venture with these words: "We hail, with much pleasure, the completion of bricks made from Topsham mud which turn out to be first rate, sample and quality, fit for the finest buildings." Alas he only managed to manufacture a few dozen bricks before calling it a day soon after in 1853. "The Topsham Brick and Tile Company" must rank as one of the shortest-lived manufacturing industries.

Then there have been those who champion the magical properties that this wondrous mud possesses when it comes to reducing facial wrinkles. Some folk will try anything to iron out a few wrinkles in order to retain their youthful appearance. Is this why seagulls never appear to age? Who knows!

And the television companies like to dig up the mud, literally as well as metaphorically. A number of film crews have visited the estuary – Blue Peter have been at least twice. Once was to cover the wonderful sight of football teams enjoying a real mudlark; another, several years later, was to watch a number of socially spirited youngsters clean up the debris that accumulates on its edges. It took almost as long to clean the volunteers up afterwards: a grand excuse for a hose down as the cameras kept on rolling.

Topsham's charm lies in its narrow streets and in its great variety of buildings with very few places where you will find rows of duplication. In the past a feature of the town was that almost every house left its front door either open or unlocked. It was almost a crime-free community where everyone knew everyone else. Another theory suggests that this was to make it easier for smugglers to escape the clutches of preventive officers in hot pursuit!

Everyone knew everyone else and out of this familiarity was born a range of nicknames, some a reflection of occupations, others based on physical traits, whilst some were deeper in their origins. There is a booklet listing them all, kept at the museum, which makes wonderful reading. There is a humour about some of the names that immediately enables you to conjure up strong mental images of these colourful characters of the past. The streets of Topsham are haunted by the memories of characters like Nippy Henson, Farty Bray, Greaser Voysey, Bird's Eye Pidsley, Fiddle Hurdle, Rocky Pilliphant, King May, Buckle Wannell, Chuggy Amos, Ranter Pym, Knowledge Voysey, Nassie Wannell, Fishy Baker, Acker Bowker and Goaty Edworthy.

Topsham has the edge on other places in the area with people needing little encouragement to see the delights of living in such an attractive place. There are buildings that were grander than the fishermen's and farm workers' cottages, some surviving, but most having changed their functions, as the days when people lived in mansions with a domestic staff are long gone. Altamira has gone, The Retreat is now flats, and others have changed considerably. Broadway House (shown opposite) is more than two centuries old, a fine and early red brick building open now as a place of refreshment. At one time it boasted a beautiful ballroom that had been added by a prosperous merchant in the seventeenth century. With its exceptionally fine staircase, it is known locally as the Home of the Doctors, because there used to be a surgery just around the corner.

Elm Grove is another one and its survival is something of a latter day miracle. Built as a substantial private dwelling, it is believed that the German air force used it as a navigational point when seeking out their targets during the Second World War. Had they been of a mind they could have easily singled it out for destruction! However, there were more strategic targets in their sights. On moonlit nights the enemy bombers used the glistening waters of the Exe Estuary to home in on Exeter, a few miles, and a minute's, flying time away.

This large white house stands on the top of the ridge rising above the River Clyst; it was designed in 1800 by the local architect, Thomas Payne.

During the First World War it was a hospital for convalescing troops. Later it was a doctor's surgery with Dr Protheroe Smith the resident GP. His brass sign is another artefact stored in that veritable treasure house, Topsham Museum. Elm Grove is now a school catering for young children.

However, from 1860 onwards most local children were educated at the public elementary school, a short distance away from Fore Street. Originally there was a master's residence. The buildings were built to accommodate up to 240 boys, 170 girls and 160 infants, a potential school attendance adding to 570 pupils. The county directory for 1914 lists the grand-sounding Fleetwood May as master; Miss Mabel Webster, girls' mistress; and Miss Ella Pugh, infants' mistress. How times have changed! The Topsham School now enjoys superb facilities on a new site in Orchard Way, opposite Topsham Library.

Matthews Hall is an important building in the social life of Topsham. Its name originates from the benefactor, Mr James Woodrow Matthews, who left a bequest in 1927 enabling this detached and rectangular building to be built. Before this the site was a farmyard; there are still old photos showing the farm's cows marching along the road. The hall was used for many activities including, in its early days, a Sunday gathering known as 'The Brotherhood.' This was a religious assembly where there was a lot of music played by the

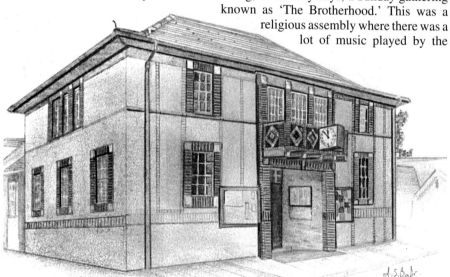

resident orchestra, cosily ensconced in their orchestra pit. This ensemble was conducted by Henry (Harry) Gould (whose construction firm built the hall); the baton that he used is now an exhibit at Topsham Museum. Sunday afternoons of yesteryear saw great crowds of people flocking into Matthews Hall for these meetings.

The Topsham Amateur Dramatic Society was formed soon after its opening, as this was the first venue where they could stage a reasonable performance. "Tillie from Bloomsbury" was their first effort. In the 1930s Harold Gould ran a cinema down in Chapel Place, a small lane (or drang) next to the Ship Aground. The Cosy Cinema was in the premises of what is now a surgical glove factory. They had a hand-cranked machine that showed silent black and white films. The programme included a Wednesday night serial, followed by a Saturday night, which guaranteed to keep people coming back to see how the story unfolded. Then when the larger venue of Matthews Hall was built he set up a cinema there, moving his projection equipment in for screenings of films. He had to build a custom-made screen for the job; after much effort, he installed a speaker system so that he could show 'talkies.' The first film to be shown there was "Palmy Days", made in 1931, which starred Eddie Cantor. It ran for 77 minutes and revealed how some shady fortune-tellers found an easy stooge in the star of the film.

The area surrounding the hall has a number of amenities where people can enjoy a range of activities, including tennis, bowls and swimming.

For a number of years Topsham's children would have been in seventh heaven at the Bon-Bon, an aptly named sweetshop at 78 Fore Street. Although it has the appearance of an ancient building, the Tudor frontage is not genuine. But all things change with time; now it's a ladies' clothes shop (Courtenay).

Many years ago it was home to members of the Swain family. Their lot in life was for each of them to bear the nickname of 'Tacker'. They were a family of builders who gave the building its distinctive appearance.

The confectionery business originated farther along the road. Started by the Fitzwalters, it was taken over by the Pidsleys. Eventually Maud Gliddon took on the business. She was a livewire involved in many local organisations: she started the Trefoil Guild in Topsham; and she was a Girl Guide leader, so was always active. Hilda Wannell took over from her; after that, it ceased to be a shop. The Harveys moved into Topsham and bought the business, transferring the sweetshop to 78 Fore Street. His dairy later became the Amadeus Restaurant and in its lifetime carried a painting of the great Wolfgang Amadeus Mozart on the frontage, high above the entrance. Number 62 Fore Street later became "Place Setting", a place to buy all the necessaries for setting out an inviting dining table.

On the same side of Fore Street, but running up to the junction with Exeter Road and Station Road, is a group of attractive buildings that are also shops. Several buildings in the town have been owned by charities; these fall into that category. 'The Church Lands and Others' owned two buildings in this cluster. Unfortunately these two cottages were destroyed by fire. Two fishermen lived in the corner property, their names being Matthews and Hammett. They used to catch fish, such as dabs, or whatever they could net, and then go around the streets of Topsham selling them.

Let's hope their language was mellower than some of the ones that hung around the Lighter! One local gentleman, of some wealth, was shocked at the strong language that he heard, so he built the Fishermen's Rest, a place he hoped they would meet in so that their swearing and cussing would no longer fall on delicate ears. This building became known as Raleigh Hall; it was subsequently used by the Liberals as their headquarters. A further change of use saw it become Topsham Library, but another, long overdue, change saw the library move to newer premises in Nelson Close. Meanwhile, this building has seen others come and go, including a heating firm. Should there ever be an inquest into the past of this building, it has a head start. The present incumbent is Elizabeth Ann Earland, the HM coroner for Exeter and Greater Devon. Previously Richard van Oppen held this position. A short distance away, his home is the attractive Drake's Cottage, notable for its unusual ceiling which depicts various historic buildings in Topsham.

Near it is Shell House, which dates back to 1695, with a claim to fame in that its own ceiling is reputed to be the work of the celebrated Grinling Gibbons.

Next door to Raleigh Hall, used to be Freddie Chown, a greengrocer who followed that time-honoured tradition of not only growing all his own produce, but also loading up his bicycle to hawk his wares around the streets of Topsham. His wife ran the shop.

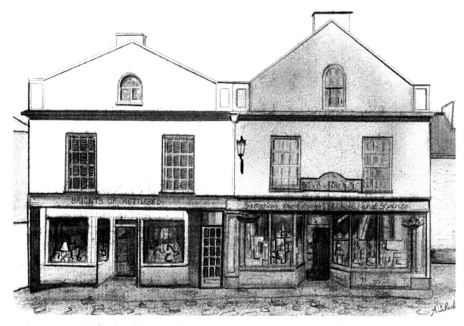

There are still several family businesses in Topsham, some of which have traded for many generations. Since this book was first published in 1994, inevitably there have been many changes in Topsham. This pair of buildings includes 'Brights of Nettlebed', this being named after a small village between Reading and High Wycombe; it has since become a charity shop for the Devon Air Ambulance. Many years ago it was a draper's shop run by the husband and wife team of Dearie and Pansy Medley. Follically challenged, Dearie was, as a Topsham saying would have it, "As bald as a bladder of lard!"

The adjacent premises, shown in the drawing as W A Nott, later became the appropriately named Customs House, a gallery, antiques shop and café. It used to be the original Customs House. If you walk along Underway, at the back of these properties, you will see an attractive sign of a paddle steamer with the words 'Established 1876 Ships Food Stores'. It is surprising how many people have walked this way so often without ever looking up to see it.

There is another in Fore Street that is shown here with the words 'Topsham Supply Stores–1890'. If you haven't spotted it yet, keep a look out for it next time you are shopping in Topsham. The firm that traded here, years ago, was Wilson Stores, an Exmouth firm. Frank Tilke worked for them and he was a familiar sight in Topsham, going around and taking orders for groceries. Then he had the task of making them up and delivering them.

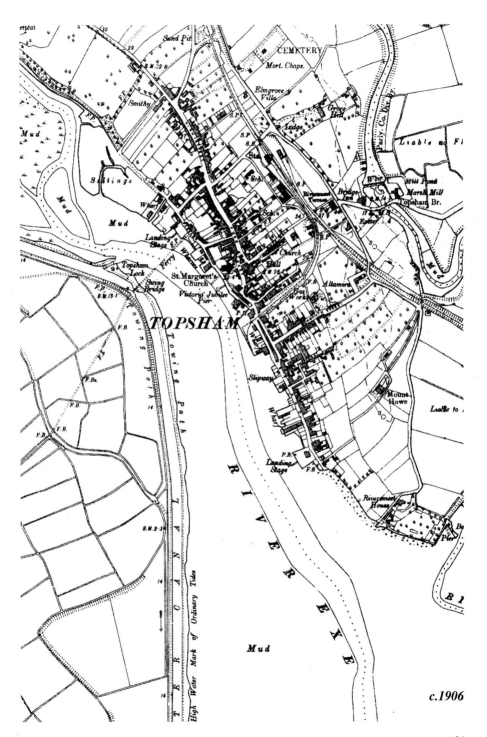

c.1906

As we complete our trip around the town, we have yet to mention one of the most important shops in Topsham – the post office! Over the years it has expanded to sell gift items, cards, and even attractive little books (like this one!), In the days when it was a much smaller concern, it had a side door in Major-field Road for the exclusive use of the town's four postmen. There was even a little fire to keep them warm in winter.

Topsham is a town steeped in history, and proud of its past. This is reflected in many ways; the names of the pubs, the marvellous museum, the enthusiastic way in which

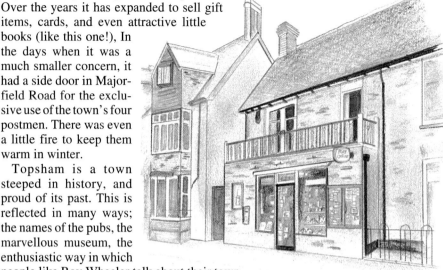

people like Roy Wheeler talk about their town and also in the Topsham News Mural. As a plaque below it states: 'This mural was painted by Kathryn Wragg and commissioned by Sue and Roger Bendell. It depicts River Exe Salmon Fishing, which was a thriving industry from the historic port of Topsham.' Although this branch of the newsagents has since closed to become a ladies' clothes and fashion accessories shop, the sentiment still holds good. It mirrors the depth of local pride, even deeper than the famous Topsham mud. May that spirit long prevail!